3/11

5.15
Lexile: ___1340L___

AR/BL: _____

AR Points: _____

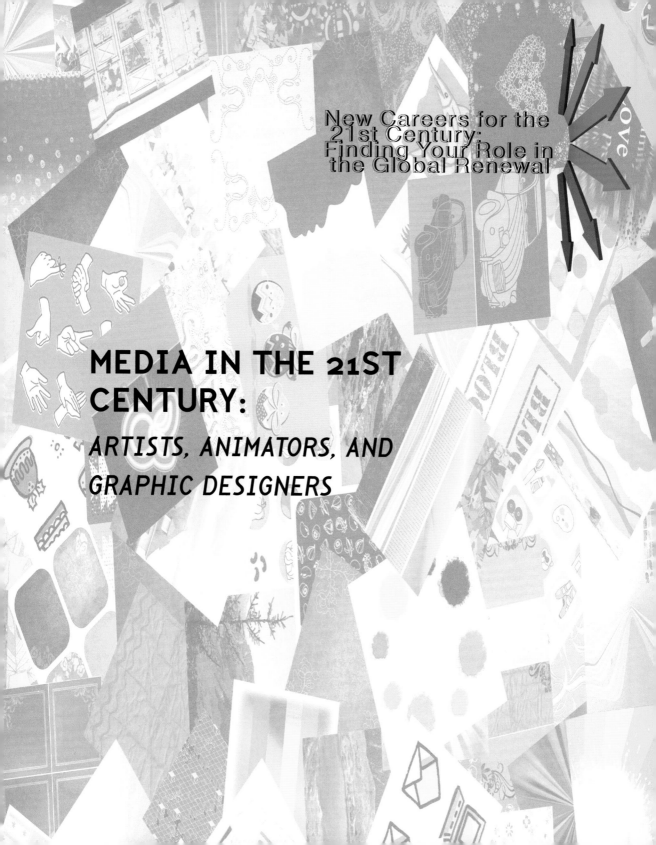

New Careers for the
21st Century:
Finding Your Role in
the Global Renewal

MEDIA IN THE 21ST CENTURY:

ARTISTS, ANIMATORS, AND

GRAPHIC DESIGNERS

New Careers for the 21st Century: Finding Your Role in the Global Renewal

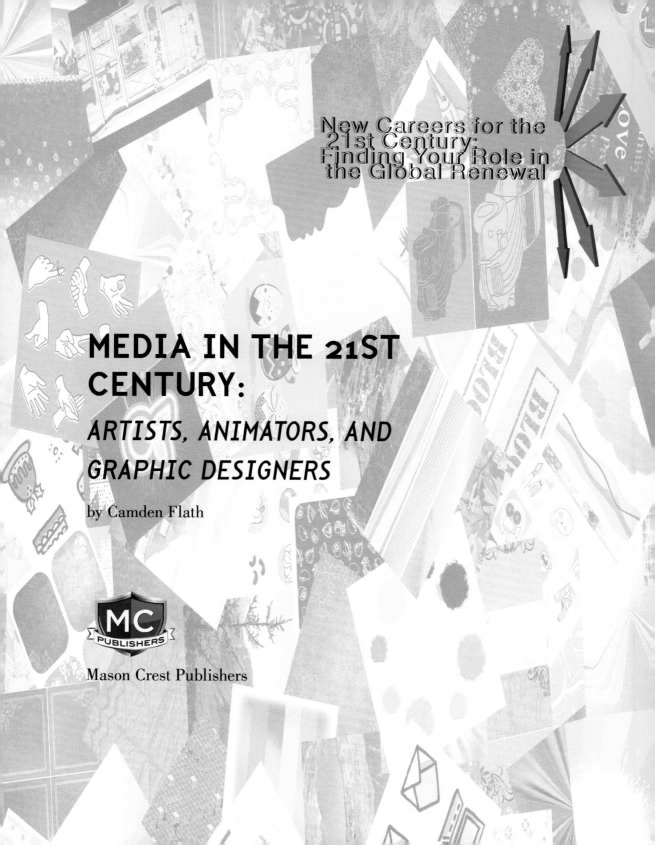

New Careers for the 21st Century: Finding Your Role in the Global Renewal

MEDIA IN THE 21ST CENTURY:

ARTISTS, ANIMATORS, AND GRAPHIC DESIGNERS

by Camden Flath

MC PUBLISHERS

Mason Crest Publishers

MEDIA IN THE 21ST CENTURY:
ARTISTS, ANIMATORS, AND GRAPHIC DESIGNERS

MASON CREST PUBLISHERS INC.
370 Reed Road
Broomall, Pennsylvania 19008
(866)MCP-BOOK (toll free)
www.masoncrest.com

First Printing
9 8 7 6 5 4 3 2 1

Library of Congress Cataloging-in-Publication Data

Flath, Camden, 1987–
    Media in the 21st century : artists, animators, and graphic designers / by Camden Flath. — 1st ed.
        p. cm. — (New careers for the 21st century)
    Includes bibliographical references and index.
    ISBN 978-1-4222-1816-7   ISBN 978-1-4222-1811-2 (series)
    ISBN 978-1-4222-2037-5 (ppb) ISBN 978-1-4222-2032-0 (series ppb)
    1. Artists—Vocational guidance—Juvenile literature. I. Title. II. Title: Media in the twenty-first century : artists, animators, and graphic designers.
    N8350.F58 2011
    741.6023—dc21
                                                    2010014935

Produced by Harding House Publishing Service, Inc.
www.hardinghousepages.com
Interior design by MK Bassett-Harvey.
Cover design by Torque Advertising + Design.
Printed in USA by Bang Printing.

CONTENTS

INTRODUCTION

Be careful as you begin to plan your career.

To get yourself in the best position to begin the career of your dreams, you need to know what the "green world" will look like and what jobs will be created and what jobs will become obsolete. Just think, according to the Bureau of Labor Statistics, the following jobs are expected to severely decline by 2012:

- word processors and data-entry keyers

- stock clerks and order fillers

- secretaries

- electrical and electronic equipment assemblers

- computer operators

- telephone operators

- postal service mail sorters and processing-machine operators

- travel agents

These are just a few of the positions that will decrease or become obsolete as we move forward into the century.

You need to know what the future jobs will be. How do you find them? One way is to look where money is being invested. Many firms and corporations are now making investments in startup and research enterprises. These companies may become the "Microsoft" and "Apple" of the twenty-first century. Look at what is being researched and what technology is needed to obtain the results.

Green world, green economy, green technology—they all say the same things: the way we do business today is changing. Every industry will be shaped by the world's new focus on creating a sustainable lifestyle, one that won't deplete our natural and economic resources.

The possibilities are unlimited. Almost any area that will conserve energy and reduce the dependency on fossil fuels is open to new and exciting career paths. Many of these positions have not even been identified yet and will only come to light as the technology progresses and new discoveries are made in the way we use that technology. And the best part about this is that our government is behind us. The U.S. government wants to help you get the education and training you'll need to succeed and grow in this new and changing economy. The U.S. Department of Labor has launched a series of initiatives to support and promote green job creation. To view the report, visit: www.dol.gov/dol/green/earthday_reportA.pdf.

The time to decide on your future is now. This series, NEW CAREERS FOR THE 21ST CENTURY: FINDING YOUR ROLE IN THE GLOBAL RENEWAL, can act as the first step toward your continued education, training, and career path decisions. Take the first steps that will lead you—and the planet—to a productive and sustainable future.

Mike Puglisi
Department of Labor, District I Director (New York/New Jersey)
IAWP (International Association of Workforce Professionals)

Where the spirit does not work with the hand, there is no art.

—Leonardo DaVinci

ABOUT THE QUOTE

If you have artistic skills, you have an important talent that could very well help you earn a living. Keep in mind, though, that technical artistic skill is not the same as "art"—and be aware of which is most important to you. We usually think of "art" as something that involves both skill and "spirit," the unique expression of an important message for the rest of humanity. Most artists, particularly beginning artists, find that their careers require that they find a balance between the technical artistic work a customer or employer pays them to do—and the true art that is a product of both their "spirit" and their "hand."

CHAPTER 1
WHAT DO ARTISTS, ANIMATORS, & GRAPHIC DESIGNERS DO?

WORDS TO KNOW

multimedia: Involving more than one form of communication (such as sound, type, video, etc.)

promotional: The act of furthering the growth or development of something, especially the sale of merchandise through advertising, publicity, or discounting.

franchises: The right or license granted to an individual, business, or group to market a company's goods or services in a particular territory.

synonymous: Meaning the same thing as.

The early twenty-first century is a time of great change in the world. In entertainment, more and more movies are made that are entirely animated using computers, video games with highly detailed graphics are selling millions of copies, and more impressive digital special effects are making their way into a growing number of television shows and films. In business, companies are moving toward online business plans, distributing content and products through the Internet. Because of the Internet, consumers have more choices than ever when it comes to deciding what to buy and where to buy it, while advertisers are working harder to reach smaller groups of consumers online. Increasingly, people are getting information about current events, entertainment, sports, and a variety of other subjects online.

In each of these cases, artists are working hard to create eye-catching, awe-inspiring, attention-grabbing visual content to entice viewers, players, or consumers. Changes in the entertainment we want, the ways businesses try to reach customers, and how we get our information in the twenty-first century will all allow for new career opportunities for interested, talented job seekers.

Your generation will be the working professionals of the future. Finding work that both suits you and is in line with the changing needs of the world around you can be a great way to find a satisfying, interesting, and rewarding career. Considering the ways in which the world will be different tomorrow than it is today can be a good place to start when thinking about your professional future. Which careers will be more important than others? Where is the need for skilled workers greatest?

In the next few years, some careers are projected to take a more prominent role than others. Careers in art, animation, and graphic design are among the job paths that will be growing steadily in the early part of the twenty-first century. The United

States Bureau of Statistics predicts that employment in these industries is likely to grow as fast or slightly faster than the average rate of all industries taken together.

ARTISTS AND ANIMATORS

Artists use their skills to create art that communicates a message, idea, thought, or feeling. They use many different materials and methods. Some artists may use paint, while others sculpt using clay. Some illustrators may draw with pencils and pens on paper, while others may use computers to create their work. Some artists create art in a variety of styles, depending on the needs of the project.

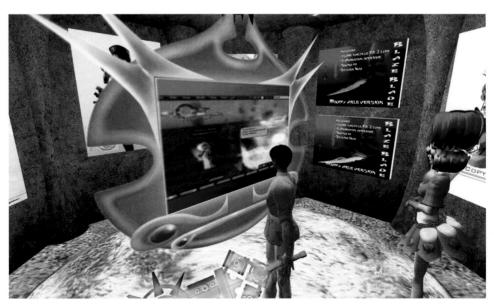

Complex computer animation has become commonplace in movies, video games, and even some television programs.

Multimedia artists and animators work to create special effects, images, or animation for use in film, video, video games, or other electronic media. These artists and animators work mostly in industries that rely heavily on visual media, including motion pictures, videos, and advertising, among others. Drawing by hand or using computers, artists create the visual images that become the animation and special effects seen in television, film, and in video games.

Some artists working in these industries will draw images called storyboards in order to help them plan their work, as well as to receive and discuss ideas from others. Storyboards are a series of images that outline the action of a commercial, television show, or movie. Artists may create storyboards to give an advertising agency an idea of what a particular commercial will be before it's produced. The director of a film may work with an artist to create storyboards that help her to plan where to place actors and cameras.

Did You Know?
In 2008, there were 79,000 jobs in multimedia art and animation.

Using computers and working with computer programmers, many multimedia artists model a variety of objects in three dimensions. These objects can also be animated using computer software. Multimedia artists and animators work together, using this kind of software to create the special effects and 3D animation seen in many movies and games.

ILLUSTRATORS

Illustrators are artists who create the images in books and magazines, as well as other digital and print publications. They also may work on commercial products that have a visual element, such as greeting cards or calendars. A growing number of illustrators are working on projects that include digital elements or material that will be seen on the Internet. Video game developers employ illustrators to create settings or character art. Other

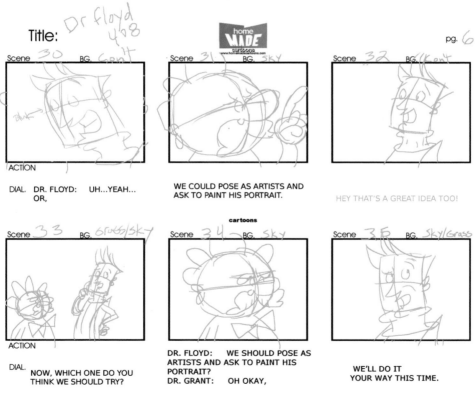

When planning a movie, television show, or even commercial, artists may create a series of sketches. These storyboards outline the plot, give a sense of the look of the final product, and can help a director plan where to place characters in a scene.

illustrators work with animators for projects created for television or film. Illustrators complete projects using computers, drawing by hand, or using a combination of the two.

CARTOONISTS

Cartoonists draw cartoons based on current events, politics, sports, or other relevant topics. While some cartoonists write their own captions or character dialogue, others work with experienced writers who create the idea for the cartoon, leaving its creation to the cartoonist. Cartoonists can benefit from having a good understanding of comedy, drama, or design, in addition to artistic skills.

ART DIRECTORS

Some artists or graphic designers become art directors after gaining experience in their occupation. Art directors create design ideas and make final design decisions for magazines, newspapers, websites, and other publications, both printed and digital. They may also work for advertising or publishing companies, guiding the visual design and artistic direction of a variety of projects and selecting which art and photography makes it into a project. Art directors often supervise artists, designers, and other production staff, as well as writers.

GRAPHIC DESIGNERS

Also known as graphic artists, graphic designers, like artists, must communicate through visual art and design. They must be able to convey messages, ideas, or feelings through a combina-

Art directors help make final decisions about the art and design of maga-zines, newspapers, websites, publications, movies, and other media.

tion of words, images, and sometimes animation. Working in both print and electronic media, graphic designers also use color, photography, and type to engage customers, voters, or Web users. Graphic designers may work to create the layout of a magazine, newspaper, or book. Others may be responsible for the design of a corporate document or report.

These designers work for a wide range of companies creating unique and eye-catching logos, product packaging, or *promotional* materials. Political campaigns, elected officials, and government organizations also employ graphic designers to get their messages to voters, donors, constituents, and citizens. As the Internet becomes a larger part of business, entertainment,

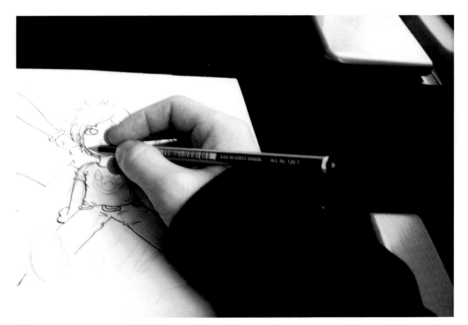

Illustrators may work with pencil and paper, but more and more illustration is being done using computers and associated technology.

and social life, a growing number of graphic designers work on the creation of material for websites, incorporating sound, video, and interactive elements into their designs. Graphic designers may also create the credits that can be seen before and after movies and television shows.

In creating their designs, graphic designers use many different computer programs. Designers use this software to create layouts, combine design elements, manipulate digital images, and more. Knowing how to use these programs to create visual designs is becoming increasingly important for graphic designers, particularly as they are creating more material that will be distributed online or digitally. Many of these programs will require that graphic designers use computers that are powerful, and often expensive. Designers will need to keep the technology that they use current if they are going to be using the latest design software on the market, something clients and employers may demand. Many new versions of design programs may require that users upgrade their computers or buy new machines altogether.

Some graphic designers will have artists or other designers working under them. These graphic designers will oversee the work done by those they supervise, giving them guidance in completing their part of a larger project, for instance. Designers who own or manage a design company may have teams of other graphic designers doing the bulk of the design work, while they work to grow the business by networking with new clients, forming relationships with other companies, and scheduling tasks. They may be involved in the beginning of a project, to give their

Real-Life Career: Lead Video Game Animator

Patrick Beaulieu helps make some of the world's most popular video games. He works as the lead animator for a major video game company, helping to create games based on multimillion dollar film and book *franchises*. Animators who work on video games create the way that the objects and characters in a game move and interact with players.

"A lot of people think working for a video game company is *synonymous* [with] playing video games all day," Patrick says. "The only people allowed to play are the game testers . . . playing the same maps about 300 times. It's not as much fun as playing at home."

Patrick started his career as a 3D artist by learning how to use computer technology and software to produce three-dimensional models of objects, scenes, and characters. After attending a design school to pursue a degree in 3D art, Patrick learned animation by working in the field. He used his technical skills to help him in his new career as an animator. His first job in animation was working at a small video game development company, teaching their animators how to create 3D art. During this time, Patrick was also in charge of animation tasks, so he was forced to learn quickly in order to be successful. "It was pretty rough for a first experience," Patrick admits. "A lot of overtime and a lot of sleepless nights . . . but I learned a lot over there. There's nothing like a demanding small company that gives a lot of responsibility so you can learn."

After spending a few years learning the ropes of 3D animation, Patrick moved jobs to one of the largest video game publisher/developers in the world, rising to become lead animator on several big-budget games. A lead animator must manage the animation team, scheduling animation assignments, making key decisions, and coming up with solutions for problems encountered along the long period of a game's development. Most games today are created with large teams working together over the course of more than a year, sometimes as long as several years. Lead animators are responsible for making sure that the animations in a game are stylistically consistent and technically sound, as well as exciting and expressive. Though his job often means hard work, long hours, and difficult technical challenges, Patrick enjoys working as part of a video game development team.

"Working on a game is very demanding," he says on Animation Arena (www.animationarena.com/video-game-animator.html). "[Animation] is a passionate field . . . work hard and come work on a video game . . . you'll have a ball."

employees instructions on how best to carry out the design, as well as in reviewing final material before publication, digital distribution, or sending it to a waiting client.

THE DESIGN PROCESS

When beginning a new project, a graphic designer must first understand the needs of her employer or client. She must consider the message her design must convey, the audience it is trying to reach, as well as its artistic merits. Graphic designers must understand how to use the tools at their disposal to create interesting, appealing designs that speak to individuals, organizations, or target markets, depending on the goals of the project. To get a sense of the audience for their design, graphic designers may meet with their clients' art directors or marketing staff. They may also conduct their own research on trends in a particular market or comparable designs. Graphic designers may also work to coordinate marketing and communication plans, while completing design or layout assignments.

Once a graphic designer understands the project—who it needs to reach and what message it needs to convey to them—he often creates a sketch of his design, in order to communicate to others (including clients and art directors) what it is he will work to produce. He may produce this outline of the design using computer software or drawing by hand. After a design is planned, and the plan is approved (if necessary), graphic designers choose the colors, artwork, photos, type, and sometimes sound or animation that work best for the project. Graphic designers decide how best to arrange these different elements so that the material they produce looks appealing while communicating its intended message

Artists may find work in a variety of industries, including comic book illustration or layout.

clearly. For example, graphic designers who produce charts and graphs for use in books and magazines often work with writers on text that is incorporated into their designs. These designers must understand how to convey various types of information visually, as well as how to cooperate with others to complete a project.

After designers are satisfied with the work they've done on a design, they will take it their client or to the art director in charge of the project, so that the work can be reviewed for approval. In some companies—particularly printing and publishing companies—graphic designers may play a larger role in deciding how a project is printed or produced. Designers may work with printers to find the best paper, ink, and printing techniques to use for a given project, for instance. They may also review a final draft of the design, making sure that the project has no apparent errors or inconsistencies before it is printed and distributed.

TWENTY-FIRST CENTURY JOBS IN ART, ANIMATION, AND GRAPHIC DESIGN

Artists, animators, and graphic designers work in a variety of industries. Here are a few examples of the possible careers in art, animation, and graphic design:

- 3D animator
- digital artist
- art director
- illustrator
- medical illustrator
- cartoonist
- graphic designer
- layout artist

Pickup Before: 8/26/2014

VOLK

8560

What Kind of Person Are You?

Career-counseling experts know that certain kinds of people do best in certain kinds of jobs. John L. Holland developed the following list of personality types and the kinds of jobs that are the best match for each type. See which one (or two) are most like you. The more you understand yourself, the better you'll be able to make a good career plan for yourself.

- Realistic personality: This kind of person likes to do practical, hands-on work. He or she will most enjoy working with materials that can be touched and manipulated, such as wood, steel, tools, and machinery. This personality type enjoys jobs that require working outdoors, but he or she does NOT enjoy jobs that require a lot of paperwork or close teamwork with others.
- Investigative personality: This personality type likes to work with ideas. He or she will enjoy jobs that require lots of thinking and researching. Jobs that require mental problem solving will be a good fit for this personality.
- Artistic personality: This type of person enjoys working with forms, designs, and patterns. She or he likes jobs that require self-expression—and that don't require following a definite set of rules.
- Social personality: Jobs that require lots of teamwork with others, as well as teaching others, are a good match for this personality type. These jobs often involve helping others in some way.
- Enterprising personality: This person will enjoy planning and starting new projects, even if that involves a degree of risk-taking. He or she is good at making decisions and leading others.
- Conventional personality: An individual with this type of personality likes to follow a clear set of procedures or routines. He or she doesn't want to be the boss but prefers to work under someone else's leadership. Jobs that require working with details and facts (more than ideas) are a good fit for this personality.

*The work will
teach you how
to do it.*

—Estonian proverb

ABOUT THE QUOTE

The only way to gain experience as an artist or designer is by creating
art and designs! It doesn't matter how prestigious your degree or job title
may be. Natural talent plays a role as well, but it can't replace practice.
The more you create drawings, illustrations, and designs, the better you
will become. Practice gives you automatic skills your talent and creativity can quickly reach for and use whenever you need to do a job.

CHAPTER 2
EDUCATION AND TRAINING

WORDS TO KNOW

postsecondary: Having to do with the education that takes place after graduation from high school.

studio: Having to do with the instruction and study concerned with the practice of drawing, painting, sculpture, printmaking, and other visual arts.

master's degree: The academic degree that is higher than a four-year bachelor's degree, but lower than a doctoral degree. Most master's degrees require two to three years of additional study after a four-year college or university program.

freelancers: People who work for themselves; they sell their services to clients, without having a long-term commitment to any single employer.

liberal arts: Studies intended to provide general knowledge and intellectual skills (rather than occupational or professional skills).

flexibility: The ability to change or adapt as circumstances require.

objectively: In a manner not influenced by emotions or personal bias.

copyeditors: People who correct and prepare a manuscript for layout and printing.

Almost all careers in art, animation, and graphic design will require some sort of degree. Whether it's a bachelor's degree from a four-year college or university with a major in design, or a two-year program from a professional school, educational experience is absolutely vital for those seeking jobs in this field in the twenty-first century. Artists, animators, and graphic designers will need to be taught how to utilize the latest technologies and techniques. Employers looking to hire artists or designers will look to an applicant's educational background to get a good sense of her skills and base of knowledge. Though it won't be the only determining factor when these employers decide to hire, education is an important part of a good foundation for any career in art, animation, or graphic design.

Artists and Animators

Education and Training

Due to the fact that their job is so technically complicated, multimedia artists and animators will likely need a bachelor's degree. *Postsecondary* schools dedicated to art and design offer aspiring multimedia artists and animators a variety of programs that focus on building the skills they will need for their future careers. These schools award certificates in a range of art specialties after students complete *studio* training, which is the basis for many of the programs that art and design postsecondary schools offer. In 2009, 300 postsecondary schools with art and design programs were accredited by the National Association of Schools of Art and Design. Many of these institutions award bachelor's or associate degrees in art.

In addition to studio training for artists learning more traditional art techniques, many art and design programs offer education in using computers to produce art or animation. Computers are increasingly used in the creation of visual art. They can be used to render objects, scenery, and characters for film, television, and video games. Some artists use computers to create their work digitally. Many careers in art and animation require educational experience and on-the-job training in using computers, sometimes including experience with particular programs.

Did You Know?

California is the state with the most working multimedia artists and animators. Many of these workers are employed by the film, television, and video industries.

Some careers in art and design will require that workers have specialized training in a particular field or subject. Medical illustrators, for instance, will need to have artistic skills in addition to an understanding of medicine, anatomy, and surgery. They must have a bachelor's degree that encompasses both art and premedical courses. Many medical illustrators go on to get a *master's degree* specifically for medical illustration. Four schools in the United States offer master's programs in medical illustration.

Most art directors begin their careers in entry-level positions in the advertising, design, film, or publishing industries, working as artists or designers. In order to be promoted to art director, an artist or designer needs to show leadership skills as well as talent for creating engaging visual material. Some art directors choose to advance their education by getting an additional degree. They may take courses in business or project management, for instance, in order to develop supervisory and financial skills.

OTHER QUALIFICATIONS

A good portfolio is a great way for up-and-coming artists to demonstrate their skills and style to potential employers. An artist's portfolio is a collection of her strongest work, something she can use to show her talents to art directors, clients, and others. Animators may distribute their work to prospective clients and employers in video or digital form. Artists and animators can build their portfolios while in art or design school, gaining artistic skills and knowledge, as well as a tool to find employment in art or animation after graduation.

An internship can also provide a good opportunity to build skills, gain experience, and observe other artists, designers, or animators. Artists can use material created in an internship in their portfolios, as well, making even a job that doesn't pay worthwhile.

ADVANCEMENT

Artists who are hired by design, publishing, or advertising firms will likely start out with what may seem like routine, low-level work. This sort of position, however, allows a young artist to gain knowledge and experience, as well as offering him an environment in which he can hone his skills. Artists working for companies for long periods of time may be promoted to supervise other artists or become art directors.

Artists who are employed in full-time positions sometimes work as *freelancers* in addition to their main job. This means that they seek additional work on a job-by-job basis, sometimes to supplement income, sometimes to build work experience or their portfolio. Some artists work as freelancers throughout their postsecondary education, allowing them to build real-world work skills while completing their degree or certification. Freelance artists will need to build a reputation for producing quality work, being professional, and meeting deadlines. A freelance artist must establish relationships with clients who can both provide her with future work and recommend her to others. A small number of freelance artists are very well known and highly sought after for their style and skills.

These students at the Vancouver Film School are working in a class for the 3D Animation and Visual Effects program.

GRAPHIC DESIGNERS

EDUCATION AND TRAINING

Most graphic designers must have a bachelor's degree in order to get their first job. A majority of employers looking to fill entry-level design positions will require that applicants hold a degree in fine arts or graphic design. These degrees are offered at many four-year colleges and universities, as well as art and design postsecondary schools. To complete their degrees, design students will take courses in commercial graphic design, printing processes, and website design, among other subjects. Many courses focus specifically on computer design, an important set of skills young graphic designers will need to utilize in their early careers. As employers search for employees who can produce visual materials in a variety of formats—for use online, in video, and in print—experience with design software will become a vital base of knowledge for graphic designers.

Graphic designers will also benefit from having a broad base of knowledge that includes *liberal arts* classes. Design students who learn about communication, business, foreign language, art history, and other subjects often use their educational experience in future careers as graphic designers.

Many professional schools offer two- and three-year associate degrees and certificates for those who want to become graphic designers. After completing these programs, graduates are qualified for low-level graphic artist positions; they may also be assistants to graphic designers. These programs allow people who may already have attended a four-year college and hold a degree in another field to learn graphic design.

At art and design schools, students may be required to complete a year of design courses before they are able to enter the regular bachelor's degree program. These courses can sometimes be completed in high school. Young people who want to attend art and design schools often have to submit a portfolio of their work as part of the application process.

Graphic designers need to be up to date with the latest technology and computer software used to create designs. Education in using computers to create visual art is available at art and design postsecondary schools, as well as at some four-year colleges and universities. These courses prepare young designers to use the tools vital to a career in graphic design. This is even more the case today, as clients, employers, and consumers demand more material delivered digitally and online, as well as in traditional print.

OTHER QUALIFICATIONS

In addition to artistic talents, graphic designers must be creative, able to communicate well with others, and willing to work to solve tough problems. Though much of their work is in the visual arts, communicating information visually, graphic designers must also be able to express their ideas to others verbally and in writing. Designers need to meet deadlines, stay on task, and schedule their time effectively. Production plans may change frequently, making *flexibility* vital for graphic designers.

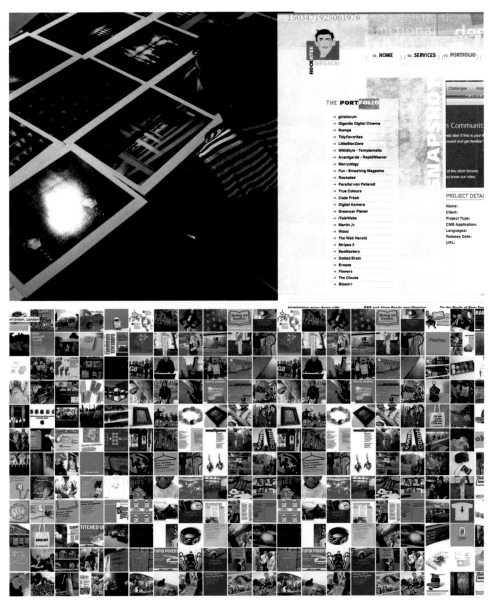

Art students and artists need to develop some type of portfolio that exhibits their best work for prospective employers. There are many different ways to create and show a portfolio.

Graphic designers should create a portfolio of their work that they can show to prospective employers and clients. Many people looking to hire a graphic designer make their decision based on a designer's portfolio. Designers who have a critical eye and can view their work as *objectively* as is possible will find that their portfolio is stronger for the attention to detail.

ADVANCEMENT

Graphic designers just starting their careers will usually need between one and three years to gain enough work experience to move to higher positions in their field. Those graphic designers working in large companies may be promoted to become lead designers, art or creative directors, or managers. Graphic designers who have built significant experience and skill may choose to start their own design company or pursue a more specialized design career (perhaps requiring further education or training).

Some workers may leave commercial graphic design to pursue a career teaching art or design. These designers may continue to do some graphic design work in addition to their teaching responsibilities, operating their own design companies or consulting with clients on a freelance basis.

CAREERS IN GRAPHIC DESIGN: LAYOUT ARTIST

Also known as desktop publishers, layout artists use computer software to design pages in books and magazines. They combine text, photography, visual art, and other images to create page designs that will be printed and published. Layout artists may work on books, magazines, calendars, newspapers, or other publications and printed products. These workers may also work on creating some of the graphic material used in their designs, including charts, graphs, or some text. They must make sure that information, both in text and visual art, is presented in an appealing and accessible way, always keeping in mind the audience for which the material is being produced. Some layout artists will also work as *copyeditors*, graphic designers, or have knowledge of the printing process. Smaller publishing or design firms may have layout artists performing a variety of tasks in the course of a single project.

Did You Know?

Layout artists held around 26,000 jobs in 2008. Employment of layout artists is projected to decline by more than 20 percent through 2018, as more layout responsibilities are taken by people in other positions (such as graphic designers).

WORK ENVIRONMENT

Layout artists mostly work in offices at computers. The majority of layout artists work a standard forty-hour workweek. They may have to work nights or weekends if a busy production schedule demands it in order to meet a deadline. As is the case with many workers in the publishing and publishing services industries, layout artists may find working under deadlines stressful or burdensome. In addition, due to the fact that almost all layout work is done using computers, layout artists may find themselves with back pain, eyestrain, or other physical discomforts caused by working long hours at a computer desk.

EDUCATION AND TRAINING

Generally, layout artists don't need a specific educational background in order to get a job in the field. Many people learn layout techniques by teaching themselves, observing someone in the workplace, or taking a course online. A degree in an art- or design-related subject, however, can help layout artists compete in the job market. Many graphic design degrees offer education on using layout design software.

EMPLOYMENT

According to the Bureau of Labor Statistics, employment of layout artists is expected to decline over the next few years. Many layout artist positions are being integrated into other jobs, such

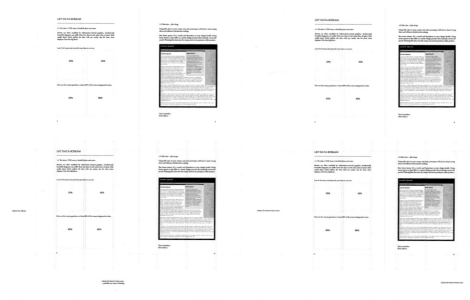

Layout artists use computers to design and set-up the pages of books and magazines.

If You Have a Realistic or Conventional Personality . . .

Being an artist, animator, or graphic artist may not be the best career choice for you. These careers do not allow you to physically handle your work product the way some other career choices will. Most artists spend most of their time inside, sitting at a desk. Their work tends to be different each day, rather than following a set, predictable routine.

If You Have an Investigative Personality . . .

Because almost all organizations in today's world require websites, you might enjoy creating web designs or diagrams for medical facility, a scientific research company, or an engineering firm. This would allow you to be in a setting that focuses on studying and solving math or science problems—and you would not be in a position where you were expected to sell things or persuade people of anything. If you see yourself as precise, scientific, and intellectual—AND you want to create designs, look for a job connected with science, medicine, or engineering where you will be able to do both.

as graphic design or editing. As technology advances, layout software becomes easier to use, eliminating the demand for experts. In addition, cut backs in the publishing industry have hurt employment of layout artists.

Though job prospects are likely to be hard to come by for layout artists seeking to enter the field, those with a background in design, as well as in computer technology and software, have the best chance of gaining employment as layout artists. An understanding of web design and publishing for the Internet will also be key skills for layout artists seeking to broaden their appeal to employers. Layout artists who don't limit their skill set to traditional print publishing tasks will be the most competitive job seekers in their field.

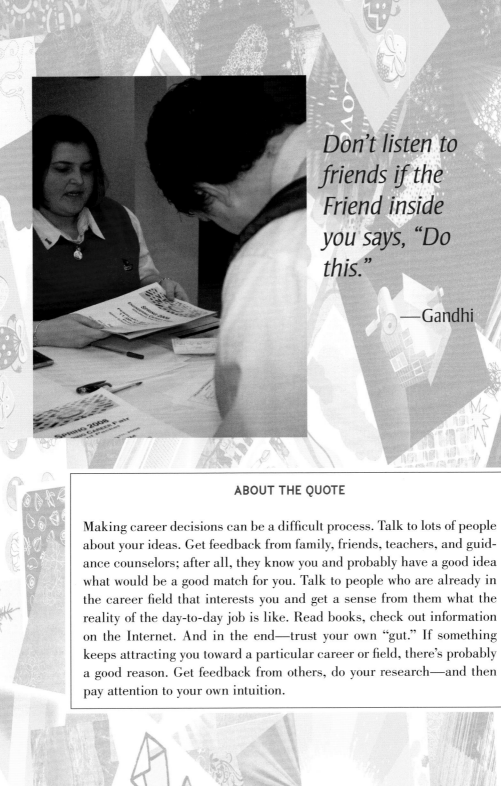

Don't listen to friends if the Friend inside you says, "Do this."

—Gandhi

ABOUT THE QUOTE

Making career decisions can be a difficult process. Talk to lots of people about your ideas. Get feedback from family, friends, teachers, and guidance counselors; after all, they know you and probably have a good idea what would be a good match for you. Talk to people who are already in the career field that interests you and get a sense from them what the reality of the day-to-day job is like. Read books, check out information on the Internet. And in the end—trust your own "gut." If something keeps attracting you toward a particular career or field, there's probably a good reason. Get feedback from others, do your research—and then pay attention to your own intuition.

CHAPTER 3
JOB OPPORTUNITIES FOR ARTISTS, ANIMATORS, & GRAPHIC DESIGNERS

WORDS TO KNOW

Prepress services: The work that is required to prepare digital text and images for printing. Prepress tasks will vary depending on how complex the files are and what the printing method will be, but they may include double-checking fonts; making sure graphics are in the right format; preparing artwork; creating color separations; adding crop marks; trapping, imposition, and production of proofs; and obtaining film for creating printing plates. Some prepress tasks, such as trapping and proofs, are best handled by a commercial printer. Hand-in-hand with prepress goes the process that's called "preflight." A preflight checklist is simply a final check to insure that you've done your prepress tasks.

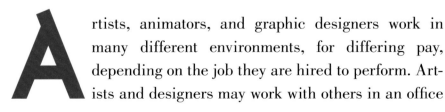

Artists, animators, and graphic designers work in many different environments, for differing pay, depending on the job they are hired to perform. Artists and designers may work with others in an office or on their own at home, as low-level graphic design assistants or as art directors. For many, the wide variety of opportunities in art, animation, or graphic design make an already interesting, creative career all the more desirable.

Artists and Animators

Work Environment

While many traditional artists work alone or with a group in open studio spaces located in office buildings or warehouses, multimedia artists and animators often work in offices at computers. Publishing, advertising, or design companies often employ artists and animators, expecting them to work a standard forty-hour workweek. Some artists and animators will need to work overtime in order to meet deadlines.

Artists and animators may also be self-employed, working for clients on specific projects, often for a short period of time. These workers can choose which hours they work, as well as where they complete assignments. Self-employment can often be difficult, however. Self-employed artists and animators must search for new work on a regular basis, while continuing to meet deadlines. They must build their reputation for providing solid work in a timely manner. Meeting the demands of current clients while searching for additional clients can make self-employment difficult for many artists and animators.

Whether self-employed or salaried, multimedia artists and animators do much of their work using computer software. Long hours sitting at an office desk, looking at a computer screen, can cause these workers (and others who use computers regularly) back pain, fatigue, or eyestrain.

EMPLOYMENT

Of the 221,900 artists working in 2008, 79,000 were multimedia artists or animators. These artists and animators worked in a wide variety of industries. Multimedia artists and animators worked in the publishing, film, and advertising industries, as well as many computer-based design fields.

Sixty percent of the 221,900 working artists were self-employed, including many multimedia artists and animators.

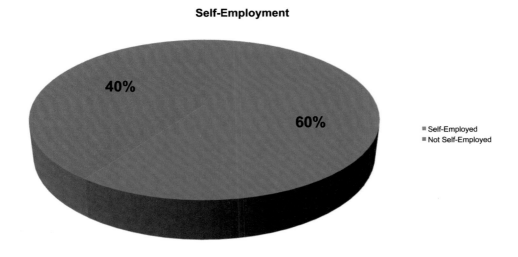

Self-Employment

40%

60%

■ Self-Employed
■ Not Self-Employed

In 2008, 60 percent of artists were self-employed. Of the 40 percent of artists who were not self-employed, many worked for advertising and related services; newspaper, periodical, book, and software publishers; motion picture and video industries; specialized design services; and computer systems design and related services.

Self-employed artists and animators sell their services (in this case, their ability to produce art and animation) to companies that need them. Many of the same kinds of industries that employ artists and animators on a full-time, salaried basis also hire self-employed artists.

In 2008, employment for artists was distributed as follows:

art directors	84,200
multimedia artists and animators	79,000
fine artists, including painters, sculptors, and illustrators	23,600
craft artists	13,600
artists and related workers, all other	21,500

EARNINGS

According to the Department of Labor, Bureau of Labor Statistics, in 2008, the average yearly earnings of salaried multimedia artists and animators were just above $56,000. The highest-paid 10 percent of multimedia artists and animators made annual earnings of more than $100,000, whereas the lowest-paid 10 percent had an average annual income of around $31,500. The middle 50 percent of salaried artists and animators earned an average between $41,700 and $77,000 each year. Artists and animators working in the film or video industries earned an average of around $65,000. Those working in advertising earned an average of $52,500 each year.

The earnings of self-employed artists can be very different from one worker to another, making average yearly earnings

2010 Estimated Tax Worksheet

Keep for Your Records

1	Adjusted gross income you expect in 2010 (see instructions on page 6)	**1**
2	• If you plan to itemize deductions, enter the estimated total of your itemized deductions. • If you do not plan to itemize deductions, enter your standard deduction from page 2.	**2**
3	Subtract line 2 from line 1	**3**
4	Exemptions. Multiply $3,650 by the number of personal exemptions	**4**
5	Subtract line 4 from line 3	**5**
6	**Tax.** Figure your tax on the amount on line 5 by using the **2010 Tax Rate Schedules** on page 8. **Caution:** *If you will have qualified dividends or a net capital gain, or expect to exclude or deduct foreign earned income or housing, see chapter 2 of Pub. 505 to figure the tax*	**6**
7	Alternative minimum tax from **Form 6251** or the Alternative Minimum Tax Worksheet in the Form 1040A instructions	**7**
8	Add lines 6 and 7. Add to this amount any other taxes you expect to include in the total on Form 1040, line 44, or Form 1040A, line 28	**8**
9	Credits (see instructions on page 6). **Do not** include any income tax withholding on this line .	**9**
10	Subtract line 9 from line 8. If zero or less, enter -0-	**10**
11	Self-employment tax (see instructions on page 6). Estimate of 2010 net earnings from self-employment $ ....; if **$106,800 or less,** multiply the amount by 15.3%; if **more than $106,800,** multiply the amount by 2.9%, add $13,243.20 to the result, and enter the total. **Caution:** *If you also have wages subject to social security tax or the 6.2% portion of tier 1 Railroad Retirement tax, see chapter 2 of Pub. 505 to figure the amount to enter*	**11**
12	Other taxes (see instructions on page 6)	**12**
13a	Add lines 10 through 12	**13a**
b	Earned income credit, additional child tax credit, making work pay credit, refundable education credit, and refundable credits from **Forms 4136, 5405, 8801,** and **8885** . . . . ▶	**13b**
c	**Total 2010 estimated tax.** Subtract line 13b from line 13a. If zero or less, enter -0- . . . . ▶	**13c**

14a	Multiply line 13c by 90% (66⅔% for farmers and fishermen) . . .	**14a**	
b	Enter the tax shown on your 2009 tax return (see instructions on page 6). Enter 110% of that amount if you are not a farmer or fisherman and the adjusted gross income shown on that return is more than $150,000 or, if married filing separately for 2010, more than $75,000 . . .	**14b**	
c	**Required annual payment to avoid a penalty.** Enter the **smaller** of line 14a or 14b . . . ▶		**14c**

Caution: *Generally, if you do not prepay (through income tax withholding and estimated tax payments) at least the amount on line 14c, you may owe a penalty for not paying enough estimated tax. To avoid a penalty, make sure your estimate on line 13c is as accurate as possible. Even if you pay the required annual payment, you may still owe tax when you file your return. If you prefer, you can pay the amount shown on line 13c. For details, see chapter 2 of Pub. 505.*

15	Income tax withheld and estimated to be withheld during 2010 (including income tax withholding on pensions, annuities, certain deferred income, etc.)	**15**

16a	Subtract line 15 from line 14c	**16a**	
	Is the result zero or less?		
	☐ **Yes.** Stop here. You are not required to make estimated tax payments.		
	☐ **No.** Go to line 16b.		
b	Subtract line 15 from line 13c	**16b**	
	Is the result less than $1,000?		
	☐ **Yes.** Stop here. You are not required to make estimated tax payments.		
	☐ **No.** Go to line 17 to figure your required payment.		
17	If the first payment you are required to make is due April 15, 2010, enter ¼ of line 16a (minus any 2009 overpayment that you are applying to this installment) here, and on your estimated tax payment voucher(s) if you are paying by check or money order. (**Note:** *Household employers, see instructions on page 6.*)	**17**

Self-employed artists are responsible for their own health insurance and retirement savings. They are also responsible for estimating their owed taxes since tax will probably not be automatically taken from their checks.

difficult to assess accurately. Some artists and animators who are self-employed work for a small amount of money while gaining experience in the field. This sort of payment also allows self-employed workers to gain a reputation for meeting client demands. Some experienced and well-known self-employed artists (illustrators or others with a distinct artistic style, for instance) may earn more than salaried workers. The average self-employed artist or animator, however, will likely not make as much as others who are working in salaried, full-time positions at publishing, design, or film companies. Self-employed workers must provide for their own benefits, including health and dental insurance, as well as retirement savings.

> **Did You Know?**
> In 2008, there were 286,100 jobs in graphic design.

GRAPHIC DESIGNERS

WORK ENVIRONMENT

Graphic designers work for many different kinds of companies, in many different environments. Those who working for advertising agencies or publishing companies, for example, will most likely work a standard workweek in an office setting. Designers at smaller firms, such as a design consulting company, may work more irregular schedules, sometimes working around the schedule of company clients, as well as their coworkers. They may work in a centralized company office or they may work at a home office, communicating with their coworkers electronically.

To an even greater extent, freelance graphic designers must work long, sometimes unpredictable hours in order to meet deadlines and the expectations of their clients, whether those include an evening meeting to finalize a decision or an early-morning deadline. In general, graphic designers who work as freelancers or those who freelance as design consultants will work longer hours than their peers who hold full-time, salaried positions. Freelance graphic designers have the freedom to choose when they work on assignments, but they also must contend with the need to find new work through networking and self-promotion. As is the case with many freelance careers, a graphic designer being paid by the assignment might have to work weekends, nights, or holidays. Freelance graphic designers may work from almost anywhere, using electronic communication to stay in touch with clients and employers. Some clients may want a graphic designer to work in their office so that the designer can work with a team of others.

EMPLOYMENT

The majority of graphic designers work in design services companies: advertising agencies or services firms; printing and *prepress services* companies; or book, magazine, and newspaper publishing companies. Computer systems companies employ a select number of experienced and educated designers, who create computer graphics for use in graphic user interfaces. Some graphic designers held a salaried position (either in design or outside the field) in addition to doing freelance design work. Freelance designers work for clients on a contract or job basis.

Real-Life Career: Graphic Designer

Randee Ladden hadn't planned on becoming a graphic designer and art director. When she was in college, she worked toward becoming a medical illustrator, planning to create images for medical textbooks and reports. Over time, however, Randee began working for publications aimed at broader audiences, including major newspapers. She'd taken classes on graphic design in college and began putting that experience to use in her professional life, working as a part-time freelance graphic designer. When the magazines and newspapers she'd been working for closed their doors or made severe budget cuts around 2001, Randee knew it was time to get her first full-time, salaried position. Now she works as a graphic designer and art director at a publishing services company, utilizing her freelance experience, as well as her extensive knowledge of art and design.

"I like the problem solving aspect of design," Randee says on the All Art Schools website (www.allartschools.com/faqs/graphicdesign-profile). "My philosophy has always been to make things smart and then make them pretty." No matter what kind of project she's working on, Randee knows that she has to make sure that a particular design project communicates the intended message clearly and in a way that is appealing. Randee's job is to work with her team to create the best possible work for her company's clients.

While she enjoys her creative career, Randee also says that the pressure of deadlines and production schedules can make her job stressful from time to time. Working quickly and understanding how much time you can give to any one assignment is vital to becoming a successful graphic designer. These skills are built over the course of a career, however, and young designers shouldn't be discouraged if they need time to develop their abilities.

"I'm glad I have so much experience under my belt," Randee says. "In a publishing company, the deadlines are extremely tight, and that's most challenging, because of the amount of work that we're expected to put out."

Randee says that designers need to have a good understanding of what looks good and what won't work from a visual perspective, but that it's also important to understand type and word placement. She keeps up on design trends by reading design magazines and looks for inspiration from antique shops.

These workers must pursue new work while producing material under deadline, building a reputation for quality and timely work that can lead to new assignments.

EARNINGS

According to the Bureau of Labor Statistics, the average yearly earnings for graphic designers were around $42,000 in 2008. The highest-paid 10 percent of graphic designers earned more than $74,500 each year on average. The lowest-paid 10 percent earned an average income of less than $26,000. The middle 50 percent of working graphic designers earned a yearly average income of between $32,600 and $56,600 in 2008.

In 2008, the American Institute of Graphic Arts (AIGA) reported that the average annual earnings for graphic designers employed in entry-level positions were around $35,000. Graphic designers working in staff-level positions earned $45,000 per year on average. According to AIGA, senior graphic designers—experienced workers who may supervise other graphic designers and make decisions based on their more extensive understanding of design—earned an average of around $60,000 annually. Design directors, who lead design departments and make many important creative decisions during the design process, earned $95,000 annually on average. Graphic designers who owned their own design company or had part-ownership of a design company also earned an average yearly income of $95,000. Self-employed graphic designers made average annual earnings of $57,000, according to AIGA.

May 2008 median annual wages in the industries employing the largest numbers of graphic designers were:

computer systems design and related services	$47,860
specialized design services	45,870
advertising, public relations and related services	43,540
newspaper, periodical, book, and directory publishers	36,910
printing and related support activities	36,100

If You Have an Artistic Personality . . .

Then being an artist, animator, or graphic designer is an excellent match for your personality. You'll find plenty of opportunities to express yourself, to work independently, and to come up with your own original ideas. Because so many other people working in these jobs also have artistic personalities, they've created a work environment that rewards people just like you—people who think and act creatively—which means if you have an artistic personality, you're likely to be successful (to earn money, gain respect, and make advancements) in this field.

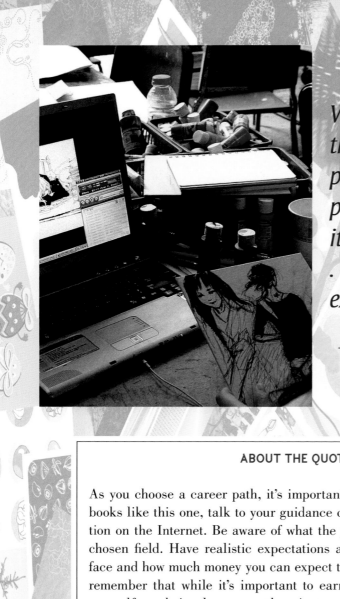

Work is more than gaining privileges and possessions; it is ongoing . . . living experience.

—Laurence G. Boldt

ABOUT THE QUOTE

As you choose a career path, it's important to do your research. Read books like this one, talk to your guidance counselor, seek out information on the Internet. Be aware of what the job outlook will be in your chosen field. Have realistic expectations about the competition you'll face and how much money you can expect to earn. In the end, however, remember that while it's important to earn enough money to support yourself, work involves more than just money. As an adult, you will spend a huge portion of your life at work, so it's very important that you enjoy what you do. You should find satisfaction at work, you should be able to know that you are contributing through your work to the human community—and you should also feel as though you have room within your job to grow and develop as a human being.

CHAPTER 4
THE FUTURE OF MULTIMEDIA ART, ANIMATION, & GRAPHIC DESIGN

Artists, animators, and graphic designers are projected to have many opportunities for employment in the next few years. As technology advances, new ways of getting information, entertainment, and advertisements to consumers will give artists and graphic designers chances to create different kinds of visual material. Animators will have increased opportunities in a range of industries, including film and television, as well as in scientific research and product design. The growing popularity of big-budget video games and high-quality online publications will provide many employment prospects in cutting-edge fields for artists, animators, and graphic designers.

Artists and Animators

The Bureau of Labor Statistics projects that employment of artists and all related workers (including a variety of careers in art, design, animation, and supporting occupations) is going to grow 12 percent by 2018. This rate of growth is about average for all careers.

Competition for these new jobs, as well as existing positions, is likely to make finding work a challenge for both new and experienced artists and animators alike. According to the Bureau of Labor Statistics, more applicants will compete for fewer jobs over the next few years, though the overall number of people employed as artists or animators will grow. Though competition is likely to make the search for work challenging for artists and animators, many employers are continually looking for creative, talented, and hardworking people.

Employment Change

As technologies advance, more and more artists are being hired to create digital and multimedia art using specialized computer software. Today, technology is an *integral* part of working as an animator in film, television, and digital

Did You Know?
The advertising and public relations industries employed more than 10,000 art directors in 2008—more than any other industry.

media. Artists and animators who have knowledge and educational experience with new ways of producing art using technology, will find that they are better positioned to seek an artistic, creative, engaging career in the twenty-first century.

With the continuing popularity of video games, movies made with computer-generated animation, and movies and TV shows with big-budget special effects, the demand for multimedia artists and animators is projected to increase over the next few years. Employment for multimedia artists and animators is going to grow at a higher rate than any other art-related occupation, by 14 percent through 2018. This means around 10,000 new jobs in the field. Though some animation (particularly traditional, hand-drawn animation) is being **outsourced** to companies outside the United States in order to keep costs down, animators are finding new industries in need of their skills. Research-and-design services, for instance, now require increasing numbers of talented and experienced animators. These animators may create 3D animated designs of a product not yet built, for example, allowing the developers of the product to review how it would look before finalizing it.

More advertising companies are hiring art directors to bring artistic focus to their work. Art directors with good project management skills, as well as the ability to work with copywriters, artists, and designers, are the most sought after by these employers. Due to cutbacks at magazine and newspaper publishers, art directors are projected to see fewer opportunities for employment or advancement in the publishing industry. Though some of these

Illustrators who can use computer technology, like drawing tablets, will have better job opportunities than those who work with pencil and paper.

companies will continue publishing, they may move to distributing their material online, where fewer art directors are employed.

Illustrators who understand how to produce their work using computers, who can create images that are ready to be used in a variety of formats, both printed and digital, will be sought after by employers more than their peers who draw by hand. Cutbacks in newspaper and magazine publishers will hurt employment for illustrators and cartoonists working in these industries. Many of these companies may move to publishing material online, perhaps keeping a smaller number of illustrators, or employing more freelance artists. Other online-only outlets, such as political websites that feature political cartoons, are employing illustrators and cartoonists, though often on a per-job basis. As the number of high-quality websites grows, talented illustrators and cartoonists may have more opportunities to have their work appear online.

Medical illustrators will be in high demand over the next several years, due to their skill and specialized training. Companies and organizations working on medical research will employ the majority of medical illustrators, though many will continue to work on medical illustration for textbooks and other educational materials.

JOB PROSPECTS

Over the next few years, the Bureau of Labor Statistics projects that competition for jobs in art or animation will be increase. As more skilled artists and animators enter the job market, the number of people seeking work is expected to grow faster than the number jobs available.

Multimedia artists and animators, as a group, have the best chances for finding employment among of all other professional artists. Though employment for all types of artists is projected to grow, employment of multimedia artists and animators is expected to have the most growth, with more new jobs added through 2018 than any other group of artists, including art directors, craft artists, and fine artists (such as painters or sculptors). Art directors are expected to have the second largest employment growth, with just under 10,000 new jobs added, a rate of 12 percent growth.

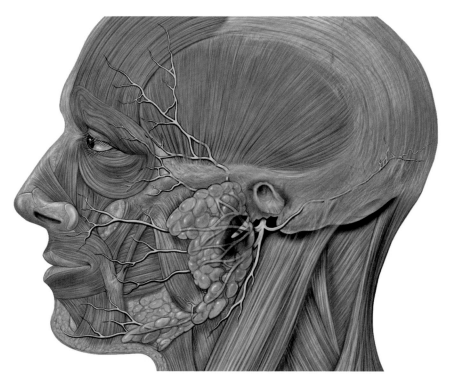

Illustrators who can work in the field of medical illustration should have excellent job opportunities over the next decade.

Graphic Designers

According to the Bureau of Labor Statistics, overall employment of graphic designers is expected to grow over the next few years. Through 2018, the number of graphic designers who have work (both freelance and salaried) is projected to grow by 13 percent. This growth is about average for all industries in the United States.

Did You Know?

The Bureau of Labor Statistics projects that there will be over 36,000 new graphic designers hired for freelance work or full-time positions in graphic design over the next few years.

Employment Change

Much of the growth in employment of graphic designers will be in advertising and industries related to digital design. Graphic designers who have a good grasp of how to use the latest technology and software to create their designs will be in demand more than those unfamiliar with these techniques. In order to be *competitive* in the job market, graphic designers must keep up with developments in these areas. Graphic designers with experience creating designs for websites and incorporating animation into their designs will also be strong candidates for many graphic design positions. Interactive elements are becoming more and more common in design as Internet access is increasingly integrated into people's lives. Advertisers will need to create more ads in a wider variety of formats for use online, creating more opportunities for graphic designers. Meanwhile, declines in many areas of the print publishing industry, particularly in employment at magazines and newspapers, will negatively impact opportunities for graphic designers creating these advertisements; there were also be fewer positions for graphic designers working at some publishing companies.

JOB PROSPECTS

Though the overall number of graphic designers who are employed will grow, designers are expected to have to compete with more people for those new jobs. The Bureau of Labor Statistics projects that the number of graphic designers looking for work, both freelance and salaried, will be greater than the number of jobs available. Graphic design is a popular career choice for many people who are creative and talented. Designers have to do their best to stand apart from the many job applicants searching for work in their field. Those who have experience working on website design or on multimedia art or animation will have the best chance of finding work as a graphic designer. Employers searching for skilled graphic designers place a premium on workers who know how to produce material for online outlets. Some graphic designers who have experience with marketing and business may be employed to create corporate communication plans, working with marketers to distribute a company's message in interesting and enticing ways.

If You Have a Social Personality . . .

You might enjoy using your artistic skills to create websites and illustrations for nonprofit organizations, schools, hospitals, and counseling services. These environments would allow you to feel like you are making a difference in the world by helping to solve some of the world's problems. You might also like working with a team of designers, people who may share your values and who are, like you, helpful, friendly, and trustworthy.

If You Have an Enterprising Personality . . .

You should use your artistic skills to move you to the top of your field, where you can be an art director or manage your own design company. These higher-level artistic careers will allow you opportunities to be in a leadership position where you can express your ambitions. Be aware, though, that there are few entry-level positions like this, so you need to be prepared to put in your time at lower levels of responsibility, proving over time both your creativity and your ability to make decisions and lead others.

FURTHER READING

Gardner, Garth. *Careers in Computer Graphics & Animation*. Chicago, Ill.: GGC Publishing, 2001.

Heller, Steven, and David Womack. *Becoming a Digital Designer: A Guide to Careers in Web, Video, Broadcast, Game and Animation Design*. Hoboken, N.J.: Wiley, 2005.

Heller, Steven, and Teresa Fernandes. *Becoming a Graphic Designer: A Guide to Careers in Design*. Hoboken, N.J.: Wiley, 2005.

Sacks, Terrance. *Opportunities in Cartooning and Animation Careers*. New York: McGraw-Hill, 2008.

Salmon, Mark. *Opportunities in Visual Arts Careers*. New York: McGraw-Hill, 2008.

FIND OUT MORE ON THE INTERNET

A Digital Dreamer—Graphic Designer Career Information. Graphic Design Schools, Jobs.
www.adigitaldreamer.com

AIGA (American Institute of Graphic Arts)
www.aiga.org

All Art Schools—Guide to Art Education and Careers
www.allartschool.com

Career Compass
www.careervoyages.gov/careercompass-main.cfm

Innovative Design Interns
www.idinterns.com

National Association of Schools of Art and Design (NASAD)
www.nasad.arts-accredit.org

DISCLAIMER

The websites listed on this page were active at the time of publication. The publisher is not responsible for websites that have changed their address or discontinued operation since the date of publication. The publisher will review and update the websites upon each reprint.

BIBLIOGRAPHY

AllArtSchools, "Career Spotlight," www.allartschools.com/faqs/graphicdesign-profile (16 February 2010).

Animation Arena, "Video Game Animator," www.animationarena.com/video-game-animator.html (16 February 2010).

United States Department of Labor, Bureau of Labor Statistics, "Artists and Related Careers," www.bls.gov/oco/ocos092.htm (15 February 2010).

United States Department of Labor, Bureau of Labor Statistics, "Desktop Publishers," www.bls.gov/oco/ocos276.htm (15 February 2010).

United States Department of Labor, Bureau of Labor Statistics, "Graphic Designers," www.bls.gov/oco/ocos090.htm (15 February 2010).

INDEX

PICTURE CREDITS

Creative Commons Attribution 2.0/2.5 Generic
        bark: pg. 54
        Ben Sutherland: pg. 24
        jjhat: pg. 38
        Made Underground: pg. 50
        net_efekt: pg. 32
        Patrick J. Lynch: pg. 56
        scuolafotografia: pg. 32
        vancouverfilmschool: pg. 29
    Attribution-No Derivative Works 2.0 Generic
        haifischmaedchen: pg. 16
        Nadia Minic: pg. 8
    Attribution-Share Alike 2.0 Generic
        And all that Malarkey: pg. 21
        bjornmeansbear: pg. 15
        guspim: pg. 32
        juhansonin: pg. 35
        tmray02: pg. 13
        Torley: pg. 11

About the Author

Camden Flath is a writer living and working in Binghamton, New York. He has a degree in English and has written several books for young people. He is interested in current political, social, and economic issues and applies those interests to his writing.

About the Consultant

Michael Puglisi is the director of the Department of Labor's Workforce New York One Stop Center in Binghamton, New York. He has also held several leadership positions in the International Association of Workforce Professionals (IAWP), a non-profit educational association exclusively dedicated to workforce professionals with a rich tradition and history of contributions to workforce excellence. IAWP members receive the tools and resources they need to effectively contribute to the workforce development system daily. By providing relevant education, timely and informative communication and valuable findings of pertinent research, IAWP equips its members with knowledge, information and practical tools for success. Through its network of local and regional chapters, IAWP is preparing its members for the challenges of tomorrow.